# Splintered Matter

Delia LaJeunesse

Splintered Matter by Delia LaJeunesse
Published by Stain'd
Denver, CO 80206

www.staindmagazine.com

© 2018 Delia LaJeunesse

All rights reserved. No portion of this book may be reproduced in any form without permission from the publisher, except as permitted by U.S. copyright law. For permissions contact:

help@staindmagazine.com

Cover by Delia LaJeunesse.

ISBN: 978-1-948850-00-1

Splintered Matter is published by Stain'd. To find out more about Stain'd Publishing, go to Staindmagazine.com or contact info@staind-magazine.com

For the cycles which move us slowly into knowing,
for the mystery that cracks through,
and for Noah, who is himself mystery.

## When Severed From Earth

As clouds slip
heat, sky, earth collides
            breaks
splintered fault lines crack my chest
spread bruises dark blue
                divide

piece by aching piece
from the rest of the organ
It could not be said this is not

                precisely why i love it

Sadness is divine when it matches
the wet bark of a tree
turned black

and when lightning vibrates
the sky along the
horizon like quivering lips
there is never more want
           for a kiss

Mouth hung open, expectant of some
warm wet to enclose
the space i've created i'm asking
that something learn to fill
that something be willing to take
up the places i've
carved out with my teeth–
so far, the clouds just stare back

at me but aren't they gorgeous
how many variations of
grey they show? Twisting

together or bending or cutting off sharp
peaks like paint and water at play on a page
and isn't there some magic
in the way they make the light longed for?

## Drip

you
gather
in the water collected
on telephone lines,
cause time
to slow down
become
spacious, silent like
where is there to go but here

morose, almost,
in resistance to all
the collapsing in on
the pause between a breath

tempting the uncertainty of the fall
(the certainty of the fall).

water pours
great handfuls all around

as those beads
bundle,
collect still
take flight from the line when
they've deemed the moment
opportune

move slow
with purpose
into the space between

## Inviolable Creatures

The moth heeds the disturbances
wraps her tiny paper
wings around my heart to
soften the impact

You are felt as an impending
loss, but in warm seasons
i have the company of moths
to brace my neck
to drink with
spidery
mouths from my eye

to bring sensation to my
lips and so

i will not feel
your absence with
the piercing wail i
could i will feel it
with the dusty warmth
of a screened porch in the
sun i will feel it
with the taste of wind on my
tongue

i will feel it with the
smell of burnt wood and
water on earth

Still, i hear you
drip your hushed words
somewhere along cool rocks
slips through memory like ice

but with the moth to
occupy my ears

the sound of your voice
will not hurt me like
it does when it rings like loss like
it does when i do not trust
that i have enough
to sustain a body

filled to the top
and spilling
i have enough

## Strung Like Orbs

you said you tasted tears on your lips
our bodies still wet and sweat in the creases

i thought to apologize but didn't

instead i opened my mouth to reveal
a pool
of the yearning obliterative
to hold on to

the extreme tenderness that makes
me think it is possible to      persevere
that it is possible
to find healing

but you cannot
hold on to warmth
the way i can only
hold your body,
salty
and hard

but can never hold
you,
anywhere
but in the brief moment of a dark
ebbing into each other's lines

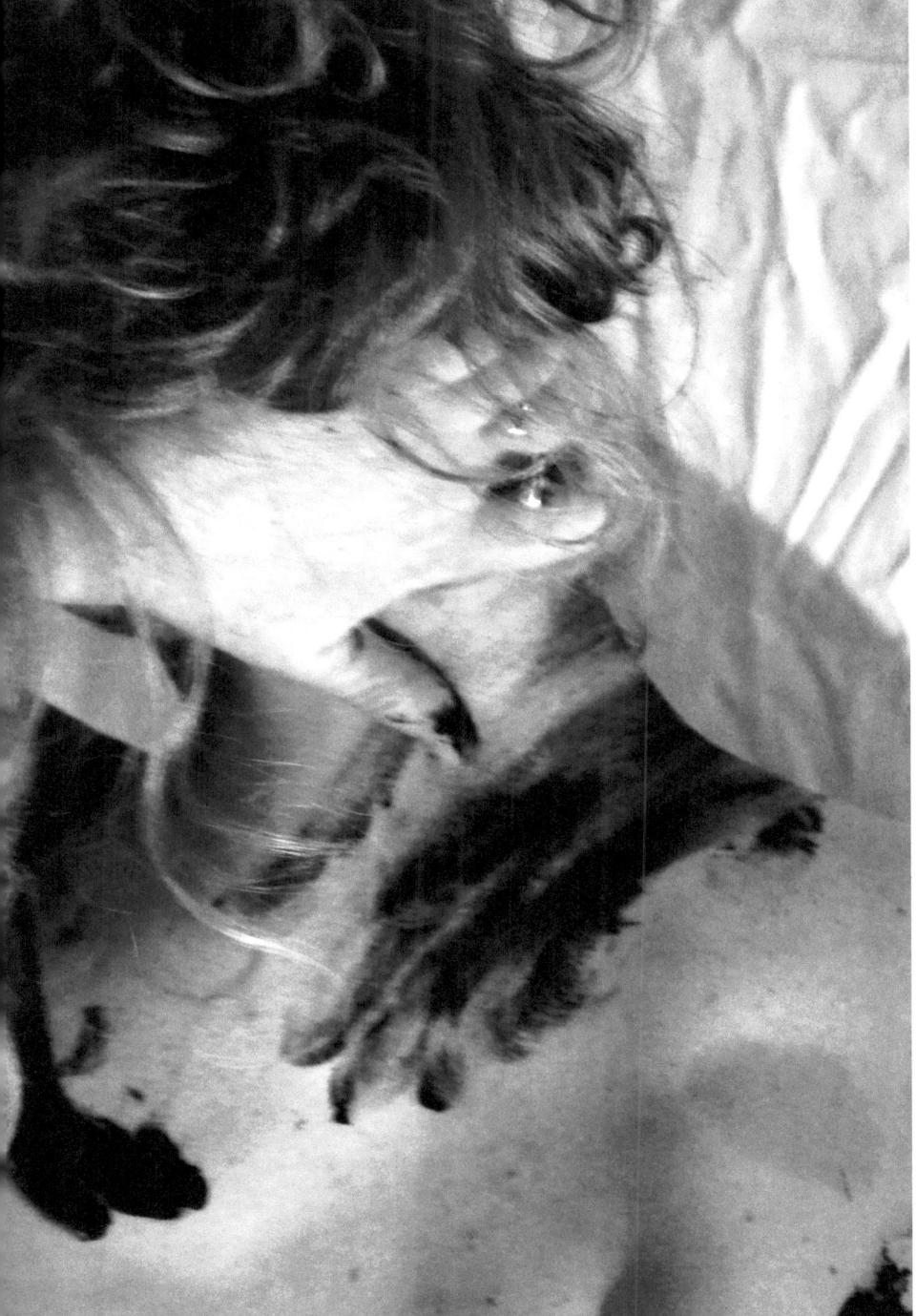

## In Keeping With Silence

                The morning
                      light

    our feet
           clasp

           one another

           cupped

    arches: a

           depiction of
                ease

## Worship, Looking For

The sun is like this:
exalting in the excellence of clouds

The golden light just before eight
illuminates the sky as wisps and tufts

orange and purple and lightning
clouds hold ground like

thighs sticky and thick like
eucalyptus—the sky bleeds

some kind of pain
a new pink

It's a wonder, then, that amidst such light
i could feel so incomprehensibly sad, tonight

the ache is heard in
echoes through my wet body

i couldn't force my mouth to budge
upward or outward or into spaciousness

with a fishing line and hook
the sky wailing

for the attention of earth
knowing how quickly it passes

The clouds crash as if to say
life takes time

vast amounts of time
it's a slow kind of build

but beauty—
is right here

it's the sky
splitting, rupturing like the shedding

of uterine lining, cells bursting
it's water rushing, it's muscles layering,

heaving, sinking
Sadness rises up at me

from every lonely face, to find
the weathered cracks in my body

seeps in, come from the concrete
sidewalks it lunges, grabs my calves

and hopes to pull me down into the
bed of the earth fractured body:

splintered matter scatters dark.
We both know, i need to pick it up

cradle it and press my lips to its temple
hold it, and carry it and know it

Who is to say if i've got the strength tonight
I do not try

(<u>gaze</u>)

sometimes
i close my eyes when it feels
as though your entire body
is the energy of water:

                female

resting on me, in me
rose water
milk

the same kind my mother used
to press to her eyes through
a warm cloth in the evenings,
seeping into the creases on her face
holding space for her eyebrow,

you are holding space
for me, your being filtered through
water such that
you come in different, steeped

sometimes
when we are like this—
i don't think with metallic fear
about my body anymore

instead occupying that anxious
space is a serene image

    of two women
who let water cup the arches of their feet
slapping sound

of wet flesh
and your body in mine

a memory:
once i looked to your face sharing my
pillow and saw the face of my sister—

i didn't know to witness
the birth of a woman
              a brief
              shadow,
              my reflected eye
mauve across the pillow,
was to hold a body through healing

if we go on like this, i will eventually heal
whether you are awake beside me or not

sometimes
i slip into a state of sorrow so immense
it's pleasurable
just as the unnamed ache for the way your body brings
my reckoning
of space between becomes pleasurable

the water evaporates
just as soon as we've let go
of one another
disjointed
become our once-hinged bodies
the rose vanished
the milk
on my tongue
just white flakes
huddling
around each taste bud
soon to fade to spit
the magic dissolved

thirsty, now
maybe lips, hair on pillow
grainy sound of sleep

sometimes
my lips are sucked to my teeth so closely
the thought of ungluing makes me cry

so i do, later, when i am alone
or nearly alone, maybe you are there too

your lips held to your teeth too
thinking about ungluing, too
of course our eye sockets are heavy
it hurts to explain to warmth
why our flesh has to let go

let the cold air of the outside world
come between, dry the liquid that's left
along our curves and bolts,
in-between spaces our bodies
sometimes take over

with my eyes closed
with your press in me, hands so
tenderly meaty that their thickness
becomes mine, and the sorrow i once
found in that is exchanged for wonder,

your golden flesh brilliantly
becomes indistinguishable from
the energy of water
with my eyes closed,
my blood pushes feminine
the image spiders across my eyelid
it is yours i am bearing witness to

## Insufficient

soggy weight of springtime
too heavy
my chest
bowed down under all
the love, all the
light, all
the enduring loneliness

when the pain
of one thing is the pain of
all things
so heavy
      yearning
built with so much ache

## She Came As Fire, You: Substratum of Lavender

Shifted
into and out of want
your long absence

the weightless arms
of your sister about mine
she smelled nothing like you

the creaking sound
my chest makes
when it breaks
when the caverns

fill with water
disorients me and
i am moved
down stream

       as if i have no roots
       of my own

It's as guttural as to
rip root from the
earth and as ancient
as moving stone

I found myself peering
beneath the rock layer
searching for clarity
what i found below
was the haunted
idea of movement

the heart ache caused by
the shift of earth the
expanse beyond welled as
a flood gnashed at the gates

i don't know which is
more true, to cry
for you or to close off
and move away from

i'm so sorry either
way i don't know how
to live in this world
if it will be so painful
to love as i do

I could never birth
a child, let sweaty head
rest on my chest

for that grief
would surely
devour me incapable
softness become
unfathomable

The world is a weight
and i have crumpled
and i wish i hadn't
seen your sister and
i wish i didn't know
about your depths

how stunningly
beautiful you remain

and i wonder how
to live like this
where the idea of
movement taunts
my being

## Circumvent

Last night somebody told me i
                emanated sadness
i wanted to defend the world
her weight
to ask out of what space he
thought the river sourced from
leapt as a stretched tongue
out from the dark spaces
that once held her close

to ask him what she must feel
as she does her daily work, carves
her fear into the surface of her skin
the structure of light, a pocked ripple,
as she weaves wet the rock layer,
stiff against her body, unadulterated
in its masculinity- and she is exposed.
A glinting body below,

to ask him what it would be
for slabs to plunge deep into the wet
blue ebbing at the dints. To have
light shot down the face of stone, an
attempt to penetrate her walls to
make sense of the deep green waters

I watch him with my fingers reached
into concavities and depressions
holes that have weighted
for touch but when i press
with my skin's lines of softness
they do not move, for me

Eyes know the water to be incendiary
how the burn of one sorrow
quickly transpires into the lick
of another the flames suck liquid,
salt remains. Thick hurt

that you could feel that much
ache so loudly be so
soft

It is the same grief that could cause
my shoulders to shake breasts wet
at the flags for a week straight; the
pitiful beauty
in the way the star of David bent
so gently toward the rainbow, make like
eyes-closed contact between sun-
worn forehead/warm shoulder

the gentle exchange of atoms
which held space for suffering
which broke me my center

the collapsed
yolk
split
bled yellow down my lines
divisive and unified
how can sorrow live like this
and still love returns gentle
and strong to the rocks

## Labor

sorrow slips sweet
into my awaiting mouth
taking pause
on my tongue

    i lay awake like this

sorrow occupies
a woman's mouth
laid out thick to listen
in the early hours
for the earth-torn

    moth

greeted
by the smudgy
light of a morning
yawning into being
she comes home
to my sacrum flattens
against the near-last
curve of my spine

wings bring into the

body at rest a faded
landscape of wet
streets surveilled by
night, cool corners, steel.

a stiff violence
regurgitated in
gentler tones through

rhythmic pulsation
of wings/to/woman

she works around the matter
of the body to integrate slow
ideas of safety, trust. the world
she filters for me through a
sure thorax, she dissolves sharp
lines, remnants of exerted force
spiritual violation/cut/bone.

settled into the coccyx
the moth calls for sorrow
brings her forth from
                the     mouth

together—space, silence

power so deep it sets the
bone on edge as if to tremble
anticipation. spine echoes, ideas
of a divine healing to come

## Flection

it is the ambiguity
that makes you so
delicate in my throat
that i'm scared of—
but wouldn't know you
without

## What Once Was Useful

the bit of red fabric
clad with gold hangs
tattered at my door

it once rested on my head
once on my mother's wall
and now blows long strands

torn red over my body
as i
pass into my room
into the air i breathe

and tells me
i know nothing
of sorrow

## Plaster

I too could be like the moon
hardly ever growing tired
of watching the inhale exhale

of your body unbound
i could cool your skin too,
plucking the hairs on your

arm a harmony, the harp
melody of silver, soft
it is slow

But lately i am neither-
soft nor slow,
and if i was i think my

hair would fall out it's
too much keeping up
with i want to see

the fracture so i run full-
force into the wall
you've presented me with

my knees crack my hips
shatter wide open casting
stones across water

## Lilted Meaning

I dreamt of your hands
how could i not they do so
bleed into my conscience


You held them before my eyes as
if you were wrapping your body
around mine the dark brown


of your knuckles were ever darker
indented inward; a spine swayed w/
                weight of pregnant belly



the nails bitten and hacked at
by that most beautiful mouth
of yours—abalone in pink


your lips so full
they could pull
me in. Hands are
maps, or dreams—

and your hands always smell
like a child's, sticky are stained
i think this means you seek

Your hands are not soft
exactly, but so calloused they've
become smooth like what they've

taken in they've held

        captive or at rest

between outside air and blood

and when you touch me
cupping my head or grabbing my
elbow, dropping down the slope of

my hips it feels like they will be able
to take up and carry whatever it is
        all that it is

that emanates through my pores
the weight the salt
the love

## Wash

I stood in the window
smiling at the woman,
heavy, hunched
older
than her body

She was too busy
pouring her grief
off in cups, slow sieve
of fat through mesh
to meet my familiar gaze

Meticulously she stores
sorrows in cupboards
for later winter nights
to chew on slowly
with her bread

Grief rises hot,
fogs the window she
stands under stowing
and quick... i disappear
into condensation

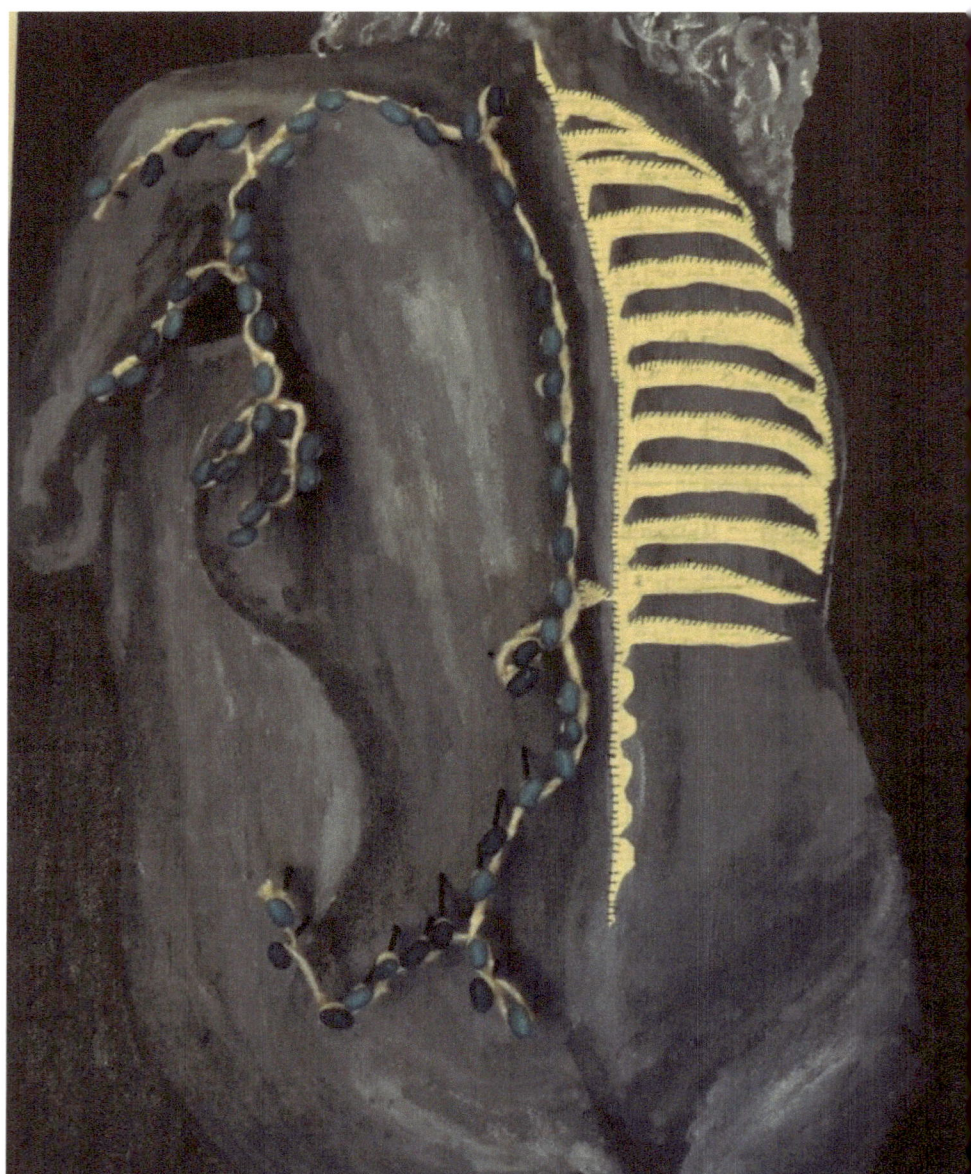

## Her Body Dried Brittle

it is such hard work
to stay open

the way the water
naturally

folds in on itself.
the collapse tends to
feel so good

## Accidental Births

i wonder what was passed down
when i slurped with wild abandon
at that witch-woman's teat

was she giving me then
the burdens i have now

knowing they're better received
folded within the soft body of love

or was it a coating of wounds
to come as if she could make me
impenetrable

milk tooth dug into softness
vicious gain of sorrow

the thin layer of milk hung
like saliva from a wolf

i can still feel the cold liquid
as my tongue swiveled out to
                                lick it up

mother please forgive me
i'm only glad i didn't
suck you dry

## Remnants of a Ghost

The air warm and unseasonable,
a bath of summer in January
whipped the wind through my abdomen

it was but a breath before
you entered into my stung
eye in your salted form

Hollowed in my arms, a vacancy of the space
you did not occupy
of my bed and anxiety like a fish
       slips in
              slapping
                     its silvery body
against my diaphragm in cold
wet whispers of worry

It is hard to reason
with a body feeling the
unidentified and unmentioned
tendency to hold space
for you, when it's not clear
you want it
a body feels that lack
molecular, it is aware

Brief interactions which cast
thick, pulsating and delicious shadows
lend me a moment of tranquility
to breathe some golden air into the
concrete of my clenched
and burdened belly

the warmth of it eases me
to the way you once broke

the metallic fast that had plotted
its way into my morning as i lay
on the pillow

washed in white sun—your
grandmother's palm—
i imagine it worn

unable to lift my head until
          you came crawling to kiss
under my chin to laugh it
off these self-inflicted miseries
and draw me back to you

Really is it any wonder
that when it rains it feels like you—
that when water licks the soils and
concretes asphalt and painted wood
when all the smells of what it takes to be
human emerge, it feels like you?

Or, how the yearning
for soft earth carries
roots to the base
of our pelvic floors
where stories
become inexplicable
just felt at the cup of the
throat, where you are

You were the first to say
there is some god in you and me
and now in the relief created
between our bodies i see,
upon you slipping

from my arms
that it is not
that you are anything new
but rather contain so much
that is ancient that your
complexion feeds the night
sky and sultry my eye draws
tethered lines through dark air
like to moon,
to you

I see the trees growing in
your ribcage and the mothers
               gathered in your eye,

i can see the built and the given
crashing together in the pits
of your shoulders where
stories mark ravines
i can see tire marks and steam

In this one human body
it is moss
braiding your back
in muscles, it is laughter
and hugs carving bones

in your foot and when
a particularly good story

some soft slip of humanity
you're bearing witness to

is coming through your face
in ashes and rivers
a part of your lip flattens

i can see the mystics
dance, there, move like
celestial bodies across
the expanse of your mouth
linking you to another world

## Harrowing Ruination of Her Altar

and now i'll let the pieces fall
one by one torn in disarray

i won't question
anymore
the sound that
longing makes

strung through
the caverns

my dark house

Photograph by Noah Kaplan, 2016

## Impermanent Beings
(Questioning Divinity)

Love
would hold us as bodies in repose
endlessly
if only we grasped the concept
of space
and moved through it like we were
made
to witness the pass of its
shadow

## Sliced, Vacant

rain hit my roof
in puckered kisses
it was so pretty i
    wanted it
        for your ears

it spent the night whispering
to me about heart ache

which before i was too sad
to feel at all,
it lay in want

now it accompanies me
is the reason i cried
when someone else spoke of
how lovely you are
how they noticed.

It was all
the inadequacy
of a
hug

The heart cannot be broken
when it's as soft
as mine

i feel always damp
and a little bruised
words (the lack of)
seep sultry
into my saturated chest

in their breadth they are stagnant
but individually each festers

in a reverberate wobble
the movement of undulation
seductive.

It pulls me
tide-like
to the shore of certainty lost

i bring my tears to bed
with me
because to awaken softly
in the night
with a kiss
on the breast
is too fragile to go untethered

it requires
the sharpness of a salted
pillowcase to remind one

unearthing comes
with the removal of notions
of always and longevity

leaving in its wake a
damp socket in the chest,
want for those comforts back
and the only sound that fits
is the rain—

>   as water tops mountains
>   in deep green the arousal
>   of occupying a cavity with
>   the subtlety of an exhale

i am cavernous at my core
stuffing words to fill spaces.

## How You Went

the strength
required to taste you
in acrid sweat and

beaded quiet
sometimes

eludes me
still

## Love's Lost Limb

The fear was brazen
the body broken down
by the want
to be all but everywhere

i walked with
no conviction, remnants
of the body i've come
to love hovered in me

over me still, beckoned
to my body, urged
a disgrace of
the fear
hoping i can hold it all

together just a little longer
to watch the flood well
pour clean
from the delta of my frame
a reason to hold up the
eyelids prone to droop

heavy,
with pending tears
breasts awaiting warm wet
of a thirsty mouth, a soft
tongue and soft gums

The fear was brazen, though
stepped out nude
on the rock of my life
             the wild currents
             the steady creation
of movement the fear

was brazen and my body
broken by it.
Humbled to the ground
to take inspiration
from the moss

the holy body
which i've come to love
how it made the jump from
rock to river

(or was it river to rock)
i crouch, watch
the fear titillate
certain
in its lasting strength
not to be carried down river

Fear, washed into the crust
formed in my eye
holding water for none
                it comes out dust
                now,

blasted this solid
salt mound to bits
fallen onto my cheek wide open

a glittery coat on a broken
jaw so broad and enduring
the night air

glances slowly, silently off
the skin there, unreceptive

to the velvety existence

of the universe,
the salt of my eye
the dust of the day another
one spent in the grips of fear

The power of its hold feels good.
In the end my clenched throat,
it's comforting

your body, or his, or mine
the salt, the eye, the fear and

the body brazen in no way
certain in nothing
empty by all counts
except for that of the fear

## Queen-Anne's Lace

sweetness come
your head pressed
my shoulder into
a state serene that
plane of my body
had not known

the sky opening
over caked earth

## Underbelly

i am not quiet

the way you are

but only because i

haven't learned


how to stand in

      light

and not look for

my shadow

## Lurched

I try to put
my body
at rest
with the breath
but my eyes
are ablaze
and wild

It occurs that
when you come
to me tonight
it will still
be in my
pupils
dilated echoes
the crazed confusion
of a deer w/ her
face cut
by branches
looking to you
to know where i am

I picked glass
with my tongue
broken mirror
shining the back
molars of a
busted jaw
scrapes on my
knees and palms
snot runs
down my face
across my knuckles
i drown
out the music

i put the mirror
in a box
i find the ledge
i've been standing on

no memory
of how to get down

I wish instead
the earth
would rise up
to meet me

i guess it has

my hands
are covered
in shimmering
mirror
the mucous
salt of my tear
duct dries
white around
it all until

my whole body
looks like
sandstone
looks like
desert floor
claimed
and sucked
in stiff by
the earth's
rocky cliff

## Recognition of God

color, in a day too bright
knuckles fix curtains
over my eyes,
subdued now in darkness

it is there i remember
that you were the first
grit between my teeth,
there from the start the
thickness on my gums
i can taste despite
the absence and the metallic
created of your yearning
                        (my yearning, your name)

## Meniscus in the Bed

the holding hurt
his arms all about me
his hand across my face
too gently

racked up in me
a stung
sorrow

the ache of want
we lay there the
seams of our bodies
tightening the gaps

he moved his hand
to the top of my throat
his fingers reached
up to my cheeks as if
to support a fallen face

how he knew i had lines
of vertical hurt plunging
their streaks of pain
in my throat
building and building in
their need for a release
      that will not come

in just that moment
must have been divined
for his palm pressed
softly into the center
of the sore

licked the wounds
that are not his fault

but that i can't stave off
for the presence of him
for the beauty of him
for the awful ache of
inexplicable grief

## Strain

keep haunting me
i like how you sound in my bones
whisking the marrow

## Body, Inarticulate

are you so ancient, then
as to be the weight of rain
which pounds into
      softness of earth
      your voice in my ear
the heat from your heart
rising steam from asphalt

i look to the pending eruption
building in the burdened sky
to learn about your constitution
to wonder about the
cascading downward
(or is it upward?)

it is like this that i feel in love
it is like this that i wonder will
my heart ever not ache will i
learn to love the impermanence
or will i, too, burst

will i simply one day be unable
to muster the strength that
keeps the soft inside intact
and what then will become

of my matter
will it still hold
the shift of sadness
under clouds
will it still hold love for you?

## The Underbrush, Returned

my body heals in licks
which is to say i need to know
how heavy the tongue can get

when sitting in silence with pain

## Dismantling of Formations

in the night i built salt caves
along the lines of your
sleeping skin
i thought you wouldn't feel
how i carved into
with the thick
of my thumb nail


your awakening brought
tears only fiercer as the
light you once brought
into the bed to warm us
was not there and the pink
of my salt shot eclipsed
shapes through my mouth


(it seems rain shed, but then—
my head is funny of late)


i apologized for the weight
apologized for no longer
bearing a gift for you


i apologized for my ego,
for being so big, but then
you acknowledged it and i
had to apologize for biting
flesh enough to draw blood.

I apologized for the silence
but you were asleep
i apologized for the wept moments
you never heard


i apologized for the way
my ear turns and you become
so suddenly far away
when you awaken
me with a kiss throughout
the fractured night
i apologized for forgetting
to see,

you.

I sit up stuck
you drift calmly
hugging my stiff and
unrelenting body
in your sleep
where my own knife
carves out columns
for my pity
in our skin. I left


the salt for you
to brush off
with the morning
Heavy,
with no known
places to go

## Smudged

in my dream i tore at her body with my teeth came at her in every

moment i could get my arms free my hair everywhere i pushed

her eyeballs in with my thumbs i screamed until the veins in

my throat emerged for she would not get out of my room she

                                      would                         not let me alone

i wonder who that girl was

i wonder if she was me

## Captor

I don't know how to pull
you from my mind
so i let you rest there
        a little while

I try hard not to be afraid
i try to stay
within the frame
of the door

but the light
on my shoulder—
i am scared
all the time

## Savage

does the spirit break
snap somewhere along the lines
and form as two new wholes

(one of want
        one of calm)


or merely bend so low
to the ground
as to taste

the dirt, to gain
some knowledge
of resilience?

## Incidence to Behold

the words of my mother
started falling out
like baby teeth:
a birth rite

## Morning, Her Disrupted Being

it seems
the body is
hell-bent on its
own destruction
the body

it bends with a
certain lack of
honor
it grovels and
scrapes its knees

it slurps and
licks heavily

and takes in
and takes in
and takes in

the body
it forgets
how to spit out
how to pull upright
to find its way when

intuition
that wolf-mouthed
matter
has been cleaved
from its chest

and moved off
shriveled up

in some
unremarkable fashion

as the body spins
wild
unrepentant and
vile towards its
own destruction

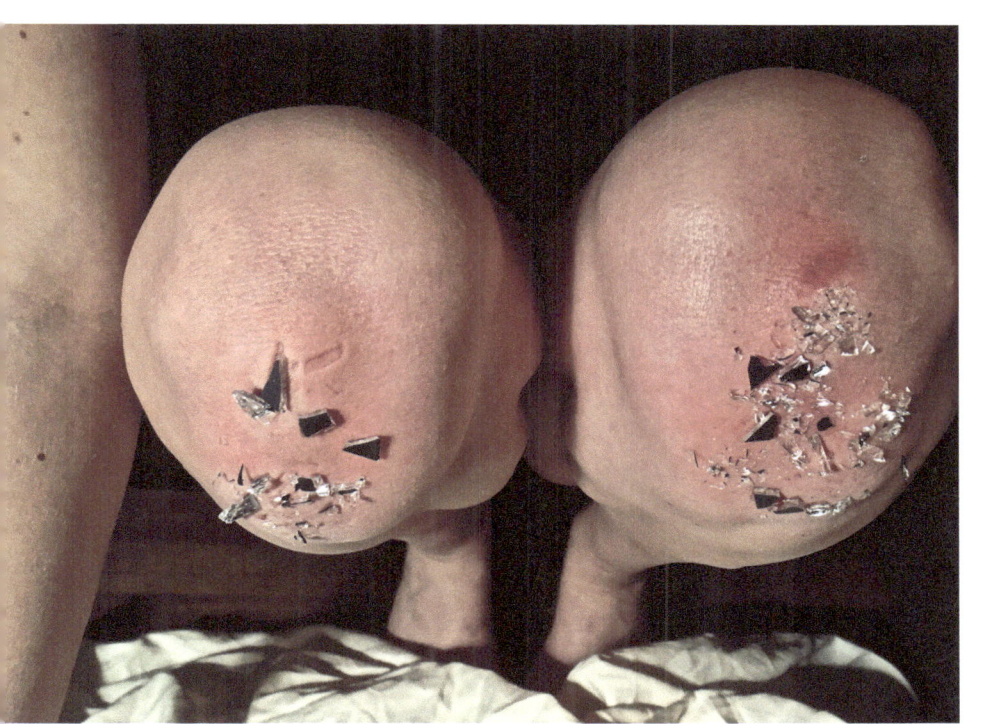

Photograph by Chad Seidel, 2017

## Barren

that silvery fish
licked up tendrils
of my blood spilled
slow into her name

i wanted
to hold her
as my body drained
of its life force

i leaned my forehead against
her cold, flaky chest
and pretended to hear
a thrum

nothing
but the swallow swallow
as she pulled red fluid
free of its veins

## Emerging of the Goddess Form

the lips split and
the chest cleaved in two—
at least each half retained
a lung

dried blossoms hung
shadows on my walls
having yet to bear witness
to the body unfolded

crumpled eyelids smooth
soon, soon.

## How We Learn To Love Again

walking backwards
over myself to get
closer to the ground
it doesn't work

i feed my ego a happy
helping of what she
says she needs and i'm
mad at her for being
the only thing
that's allowed me
to care
for it

the letting go gets harder
my body gets heavier less
able to move to
force adaptable the
ground is close in a
different way now

body weighted by stones i
dreamt my mother
rubbed the makeup
off my eye

pressed hard till i saw
yellow the way i did to
myself yesterday morning
in an exhausted anger

where i'm lacking
is so vast i can't just
fill it it is too much
insufficiency i ponder
with my eyes flashing
orange now if maybe this
isn't just the condition
of being human

i hold out hope pray
to some god it's not
                      for beauty

would then forever
be out of my grasp

## What the Body Absorbs, Reflections Absent by Definition

Will you see me stare
at the moon and think
how pretty
or will you hold the urgency

the indelible hunger
which keeps me up
looking

## What She Alone Will Do

The vision

emerges in the quiet fog left in our wake as
light dissipates gradually from the center, the eye

the woman squats hunkered in the heart of white
courtyard. sun bleached stone to crumble the walls
hardly able to stand the light she is wrapped
in black.

she is draped from head to ankle in black her
body's knowledge concealed, a sliver exposed only
by her face (my face) mostly shrouded in black
the fabric hangs loose
heavy gather
drops down lines of her neck, shoulders the belly

her knees spread wide around her frame cup the
outside ridge of her arms bare feet protrude from
black, some blue in the distance rich, but mostly
white all around them            (she is alone).

the black scrunched up her arms her wrists
weighted by metal bands hands hold textured
stone deepest brown speckled grey a pestle
                to grind with
                slow repetition
down out and up. down out up against a mortar of
the same rock the width of her feet spread to hold her,
press her weight solid against the white-hot earth

water within. wholly undisturbed by her plunging
                labor-  ing
rock scrapes rock—an eye pierces a body flinches—
stone ground with stone widens the surface for
the valley of your fears (she'll witness, hold)

the turquoise water at rest in the basin not mired or
flecked, nothing understood here about wrongdoing,
it parts a seam for her hands, and the stone she carries
within, closes over her wrist parting, sealing, parting

at the base of the stone she takes her sleep, she
does her work, the way she drips dark water w/
poised tongue over the son, over the ancestor
child to elder their heads rest upon her bosom
with precisely the same intimacy

she moves with grace into the dark ebbing about
her hips, long plunge of the belly, it traipses
through the brush of her thighs
stamps a muddied purification from armpit to pubic
mound a gathered story, garnered without language,
breath made for expansion　　　　untethered
　　　　　　　　　　　　　　　　　　deep black
　　　　　　　　　　　　　　　　　　caps her
　　　　　　　　　　　　　　　　　　washes clean

Photograph by Noah Kaplan, 2017

## Revoking Light

night
carries memories years old

i ask of the dream world
to continue to bring me the
knowledge of your body
the press on mine is ancient

the hair of your arm made its
way into my mouth

saliva pulled dark
hairs black until
your sleep was mine

        want faded to love, to care,
        to you as my son,


my chest forever held out
for the rest of your head

heavy with a day
the smell of the greatest
treasuring of my life still
impossibly, possibly to come

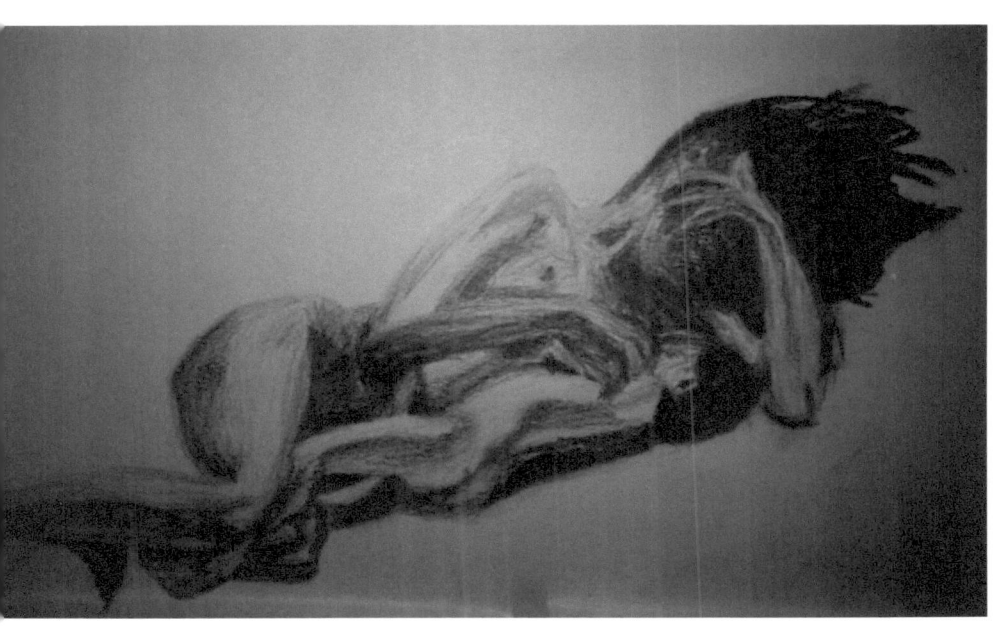

## With The Cusp of Dark, Grace

it grows deeper
and wider
the earth opening,
silty and warm

i'm sure now

i could hold space for you
with you, until our arms

collapse with fatigue

and old age
and our mouths have
nothing new to say

just old comforts to
pass back and forth like
a worn blanket

and pulled around our
shoulders, the circle,
dark womb-space.

i'm nearly sure, now

www.ingramcontent.com/pod-product-compliance
Lightning Source LLC
Chambersburg PA
CBHW042233090526
44588CB00005B/72